WOODPECKERS

DRILLING HOLES & BAGGING BUGS

Sneed B. Collard III

www.buckinghorsebooks.com

Distributed by Mountain Press Publishing Company, Missoula, MT 800-234-5308
www.mountain-press.com

Names: Collard, Sneed B., author.
Title: Woodpeckers: drilling holes and bagging bugs / Sneed B. Collard III
Description: Includes bibliographical references and index. I Missoula, MT:
Bucking Horse Books, 2018.
Identifiers: ISBN 978-0-9844460-9-4 I LCCN 2017918354
Subjects: LCSH Woodpeckers. I Birds. I Woodpeckers--Food. I Woodpeckers-
-Juvenile literature. I Birds--Juvenile literature. I Woodpeckers--Food--Juvenile
literature. I BISAC JUVENILE NONFICTION / Animals / Birds
Classification: LCC QL696.P56 .C65 2018 I DDC 598.7/2--dc23

Cover and book design, and artwork on page 12 by Kathleen Herlihy-Paoli,
Inkstone Design.
The text of this book is set in ITC Kabel.

Photography Credits
Braden G. Collard: back flap, 3 (3rd, 6th, 9th from top), 18 (right), 19 (left), 34,
44, 46 (left), 48, cut-out image of Red-naped Sapsucker on pages 20, 28, 40
Kate Davis: 1, 3 (8th from top), 31 (large), cut-out of Lewis's Woodpecker on pages
2, 12, 27, 30
U.S. Fish and Wildlife Service: 37 (Red-cockaded Woodpecker)
Public Domain color engraving of Ivory-billed Woodpeckers by R. Havell, after
drawing by John J. Audubon (first published as Plate 66 in Birds of America
by John J. Audubon, 1827-1838): 39
Front flap: Shutterstock
All other photos by Sneed B. Collard III

Front Cover: Pileated Woodpeckers
Front Flap: Red-headed Woodpecker
Back Flap: Sneed B. Collard III
Back Cover: Downy Woodpecker
Manufactured in the United States of America

10 9 8 7 6 5 4 3 2 1

Bucking Horse Books
MISSOULA, MONTANA

For Paula Kelly,
Soul Birder
Love, Sneed

CONTENTS

What's a Woodp-p-p-p-pecker?

How do you know if a bird is a woodpecker?

"Well," explains woodpecker expert Dick Hutto, "it's something standing on the side of a tree, banging its head against the trunk. Nothing else does that."

That sounds funny, but it's true. Woodpeckers are some of the easiest birds on earth to recognize. Just look at the woodpecker to your left.

- *Colorful markings on head*
- *Black-and-white body*
- *Beak like a dagger or drill*
- *Pounding into the side of a tree*

Could you mistake it for anything else? Probably not—unless, that is, you're too busy watching Shark Week or playing Minecraft to pay attention!

Woodpeckers belong to the family of birds called the Picidae (PICK-i-dee), which also includes piculets and wrynecks. There are more than 200 species of woodpeckers, piculets, and wrynecks worldwide. They live on every continent except Australia and Antarctica. About twenty-two species live in the United States and Canada, and they are some of the most exciting birds anywhere. What makes them so special? Let's, um, peck away at that.

◀ *This Hairy Woodpecker shows all the markings, color patterns, and behaviors of a typical North American woodpecker. The extra splash of red or yellow on the heads of many male woodpeckers indicates the health and age of a male. This helps females choose a mate—and can discourage other males from moving in on a male woodpecker's territory!*

It's a Peck-Peck-Pecking Machine!

The first thing everyone notices about woodpeckers is that they peck. Walk through almost any forest on a quiet spring morning, and you're likely to hear the distinctive "tap-tap-tap...tap-tap-tap" of a woodpecker pecking into a tree. And man, do they pack the equipment to do it!

Check out the Pileated Woodpecker to the right. It's North America's largest woodpecker, and that big beak ain't just for show! It is shaped into an exquisite chisel that sharpens itself. The Pileated uses it to dig, pound, and peck into dead and rotting trees.

A woodpecker's beak can strike wood at more than fifteen miles an hour. That would give any other bird—or one of us—brain damage. Not surprisingly, woodpeckers have super-cool adaptations to keep from injuring themselves. Their beaks and skull bones are specifically designed to absorb shock. Muscles attached to the tongue (see page 12) also act as a "seat belt" for the skull. Even the brains of woodpeckers are positioned to spread out any shocks that they receive.

But by now, you should be asking a key question: Why? Why do woodpeckers peck into trees so

➤Standing on the side of a tree isn't easy. Most birds have three toes facing forward and one back, but woodpeckers have two forward and two back. That helps support them as they cling to a tree trunk. Also, a woodpecker's long tail feathers, called retrices, are especially stiff. When pressed against a tree trunk or other vertical surface, they help prop up the bird as it drills feeding holes, carves out a nest, or drums for a mate.

much? Is it because they hate trees? Are they full of avian anger that they're trying to work out? Are they bored because their parents took away their video games? The answer—or answers—turn out to be simpler than that...

Meet Our Most Common Woodpeckers!

Two neighborhood woodpeckers people are likely to see are the Downy Woodpecker and the Northern Flicker. Small—and adorably cute—Downy Woodpeckers seem to adapt to most any environment with trees and plenty of insects to eat. Downies frequently visit bird feeders and are often confused with Hairy Woodpeckers (see pages 4 and 5). How do you tell them apart? Downies are smaller, and the lengths of their beaks are only about half the width of their heads. A Hairy's beak is about as long as the entire width of its head.

Like Downies, Northern Flickers are common neighborhood residents. Unlike Downies, Northern Flickers are often seen on the ground snatching up ants to eat. A Northern Flicker is most easily identified by the bold flash of orange under its wings while in flight. Also look for a white rump patch. To learn more, read "Out-of-Control Woodpecker Teenagers" on page 22.

◄ *Besides being irresistibly cute, Downy Woodpeckers adapt well to urban environments.*

➤ *The next time you see a large, grayish bird on the ground, take a closer look—it may be a Northern Flicker gobbling up ants!*

Eating Like You Mean It

One of the main reasons woodpeckers pound and drill into trees is to score a meal. Woodpeckers devour a wide variety of foods including seeds, berries, nuts, and sap. However, hands—or feathers—down, the Number One Item on most woodpecker grocery lists is insects. They especially love tasty ants and beetle grubs, and where do they find them? You guessed it—dead or sick trees.

The problem is that these insects are generally munching away *inside* of a tree, forcing woodpeckers to tear into the wood to reach their prey. Fortunately, its reinforced beak turns a woodpecker into a "one-bird wrecking crew," drilling and ripping away bark and wood to get at the juicy morsels inside. The bird, though, has another useful feeding tool.

To help them snatch their prey, most woodpeckers come equipped with amazingly long tongues. "A woodpecker's tongue is about twice as long as the bill," explains Dick Hutto. "The tongue is really interesting because it's attached to a hyoid bone, so the bone goes in and out with the tongue."

The hyoid bone of some woodpeckers is so long that it actually winds around inside the skull and

➤ *Woodpeckers such as this Hairy Woodpecker eat a variety of foods, but insects are at the top of their, ahem, grub list.*

into the bird's nostrils! You'd think that would make it hard for woodpeckers to sneeze, but I've never heard the birds complain.

A useful feature of the tongue is that it has special barbs on it. These act as little "fish hooks" to help woodpeckers snag their prey. If that isn't enough, many woodpecker tongues are extremely sticky.  Once a woodpecker has drilled a hole into a tree, it uses its long sticky tongue to probe into tiny cracks and crevices deep inside the wood. That makes a woodpecker one lean, mean insect-eating machine!

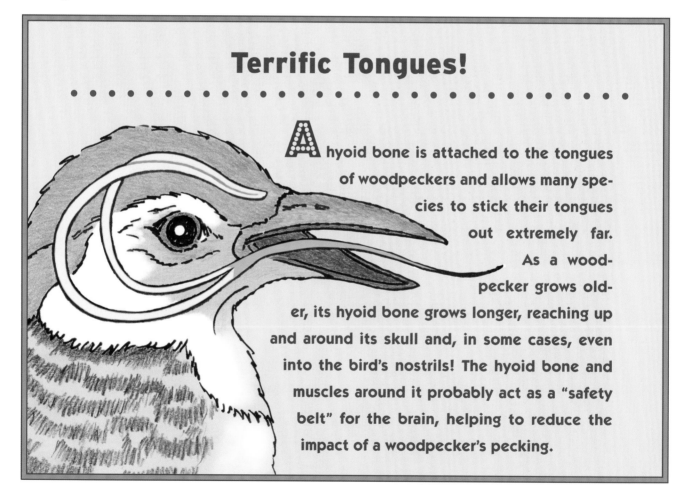

Terrific Tongues!

A hyoid bone is attached to the tongues of woodpeckers and allows many species to stick their tongues out extremely far. As a woodpecker grows older, its hyoid bone grows longer, reaching up and around its skull and, in some cases, even into the bird's nostrils! The hyoid bone and muscles around it probably act as a "safety belt" for the brain, helping to reduce the impact of a woodpecker's pecking.

Woodpeckers as Prey

As aggressive as woodpeckers are as predators, they also have to watch their tail feathers. Squirrels, birds, snakes, and other predators eat woodpecker eggs and young, and some go after adult woodpeckers themselves. In one forest area of South Carolina, Sharp-shinned Hawks killed 13 of 93 Red-headed Woodpeckers over the course of two summers. In this case, having a bright red head wasn't such a great thing after all.

◄ *Red-headed Woodpecker*

Birds with Cavities— Woodpecker Real Estate

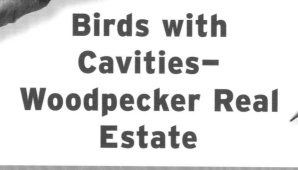

As important as food is, woodpeckers use their amazing beaks for another equally important purpose—to carve their own homes. All woodpeckers are cavity nesters. This does not mean that they live in dentists' offices! It means that they use their bills to excavate nest holes in the trunks of trees. Different kinds of woodpeckers choose different kinds of trees to nest in. Some prefer soft, rotten trees while others drill into trees that can seem as hard as concrete lamp posts.

When they aren't nesting, woodpeckers still need holes to snooze in. These roosting sites can be in live or dead trees. A Pileated Woodpecker, for instance, picks dead hollow tree trunks to roost in. The bird simply chisels entry holes into the trunk and… instant apartment! Scientists in Oregon found that each Pileated used about seven different roosting trees during a three- to ten-month period.

Woodpeckers, of course, are not the only birds to nest and roost in tree holes. What sets wood-

◄ *When this nestling Pileated finishes with this hole, chances are another animal will move into it.*

14

peckers apart is that they *dig out the holes themselves*. This makes woodpeckers kingpins of forest ecosystems. Owls, ducks, bats, and even pine martens move into Pileated nesting holes. Holes from Hairy, Three-toed, and Black-backed Woodpeckers are used by bluebirds, chickadees, wrens, and many other songbird species. What would happen without woodpeckers and their holes? Well, a lot of bird species would just be hanging out on street corners, shoplifting flies and beetle grubs, and getting into trouble with the law.

Just kidding—but you get the point.

❯ This Northern Pygmy-Owl will not only nest in a woodpecker hole—it has been known to eat woodpeckers, too. Is this where we got the phrase "having your bird and eating it too?"

❯ Wood Ducks are one of many bird species that can nest in abandoned woodpecker holes.

Would You Like that Tree Soft, Medium, or Hard?

Although most woodpeckers dig into wood, not all woodpeckers are created equal. According to Dick Hutto, Northern Flickers, Lewis's Woodpeckers, and even the big Pileateds are fairly weak excavators. These woodpeckers mostly drill into soft,

◄ *Lewis's Woodpeckers are some of the weakest excavators and rely on soft, rotten trees to build their nests.*

➤ *Downy Woodpeckers can drill into trees of medium hardness—including those that might be growing around your neighborhood.*

"cruddy" trees that are easy to tear apart. One of our common neighborhood woodpeckers, the Downy Woodpecker, can drill into trees of more medium hardness. Higher on the hardness scale comes the Hairy Woodpecker, and finally, the real "cement heads"—the Three-toed and Black-backed Woodpeckers. "They can dig into extremely hard trees," Dick explains. "You take a lodgepole, which is like a rock, and it's not that big around and they can drill a nest in there."

➤ *Three-toed Woodpeckers are real "hard heads." They can drill into trees that seem as hard as granite.*

Black-cheeked Woodpecker

Cream-colored Woodpecker

Woodpeckers Abroad

• •

Though we are fortunate to have twenty-two or so woodpecker species in the United States and Canada, most woodpeckers live in other parts of the world. About fifty-five species live in South America. Here are four that my son and I were lucky enough to see on recent adventures to Ecuador and Peru.

🖋 BLACK-CHEEKED WOODPECKER. This woodpecker ranges from Mexico down into Colombia and Ecuador. Very little is known about it, but this one was pecking away in a dry tropical forest of Ecuador.

🖋 CREAM-COLORED WOODPECKER. Thought all woodpeckers were mostly black and white? Think

Andean Flicker

Guayaquil Woodpecker

again! Perhaps the world's only creamy yellow woodpecker, this cool dude prefers seasonally flooded forests in the Amazon Basin.

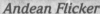 **ANDEAN FLICKER.** Unlike our Northern Flickers, Andean Flickers turn up their beaks at trees, and instead prefer wide-open, rocky places. We enjoyed watching these guys ant-hunting among Incan ruins near Cuzco, Peru.

GUAYAQUIL WOODPECKER. Like your woodpeckers big and bold? The Guayaquil Woodpecker is for you! One of a dozen large woodpeckers that resemble our Pileated Woodpecker, the Guayaquil Woodpecker lives in dry and moist forests along the coasts of Ecuador, Colombia, and Perú.

Heavy Metal Drumming– Woodpecker Communication

By now, you should be getting the idea that a woodpecker's beak is an essential tool for finding food and carving out a home. Woodpeckers, though, use their beaks for one more important purpose: communication.

To communicate, woodpeckers call to each other, sing songs, and text each other like other birds do. (Again, just kidding about the texting. Dudes, lighten up already.) But woodpeckers also do something unknown in the rest of the bird world. They drum! With rapid beak thrusts they pound on hollow trees, rain gutters—anything that will produce a loud noise.

"The drumming is species-specific," says Dick Hutto. "Just like you can tell a Yellow Warbler from a Yellow-rumped Warbler by its call, you can tell different kinds of woodpeckers by their different drumming patterns."

A Hairy Woodpecker's drumming can be heard from more than a quarter mile away. Drumming helps a male warn other males

◀ Am I high enough yet? I watched this Pileated drum against this tall snag every morning for two weeks straight.

► Every spring, Northern Flickers belt out calls until their voice boxes throb! Why? To attract mates and tell other males, "This stage—and territory—are mine!"

not to enter his territory—something scientists take advantage of.

"That's how we attract woodpeckers and tell that they're around," explains Dick. "We record their drumming and play it back. Woodpeckers will come attack the loudspeaker if they think it's another male intruding on their territories."

Drumming, though, serves one other vital purpose: it helps a male woodpecker attract a mate. Which brings us to the all-important subject of…

◄ The drumming of Red-naped Sapsuckers slows and "dribbles" away at the end of each burst.

Out-of-Control Woodpecker Teenagers

· ·

Every spring, when I am walking my kids to school, I hear raucous calls echoing through our neighborhood and the nearby woods. These calls start slow, then build in speed and volume until they sound like rock stars at the Bird-a-Palooza Outdoor Music Festival. With a little effort, it's easy to see who is making these calls—male Northern Flickers. The males sit perched on rooftops or in the highest snags belting out calls like the best lead singers.

Every lead vocalist needs instruments behind him, of course, and like other woodpeckers, flickers throw in radical drumming to back themselves up. In a furious burst of head thrusts, they pound their beaks against almost any noisy surface. In the forest, hollow trees make excellent drums, but in neighborhoods, roofs, chimneys, and rain gutters serve just as well. It's no surprise that these Heavy Metal birds are often Enemy Number One of tired parents who are trying to catch an extra hour's sleep on a Sunday morning.

➤ *At least once a year, a Northern Flicker shows up outside of my office window to get in a little drumming practice!*

Woodpecker Families

If you had to choose non-human parents—and I'm sure you've been tempted—you could do a lot worse than choosing a woodpecker mom and dad. Birds in general make outstanding parents, and woodpeckers score high marks. In most woodpecker species, once a male has attracted a female, the couple works together to carve out a nest hole, protect the eggs and hatchlings, and feed them. Some woodpeckers, though, have come up with mind-bending variations to traditional bird family life.

Acorn Woodpeckers live in family groups of up to fifteen birds. Besides eating insects, Acorn Woodpeckers depend on acorns from oak trees to survive. "Acorn Woodpeckers can apparently eat nothing BUT

◄ *Acorn Woodpeckers live in family groups and help each other raise their young. Scientists call this "cooperative breeding," and it has also been observed in Red-cockaded Woodpeckers and, less often, in Red-headed Woodpeckers.*

Cornering the Acorn Market

Acorn Woodpeckers spend huge parts of the year collecting and storing acorns—usually in trees called granaries that are riddled with thousands of storage holes. A single oak tree granary may have as many as 50,000 holes in it! Into each hole, the woodpeckers stuff a single acorn. When a better granary comes along, the birds often take advantage of it. In one unused house, Acorn Woodpeckers stuffed 62,264 acorns into the door and window casings. Another group stashed almost 500 pounds of acorns into an old water tank! Utility companies often have to replace wooden telephone poles that the woodpeckers use as their personal acorn cupboards.

➤ *Telephone poles serve as important granaries for Acorn Woodpeckers in California.*

acorns for several weeks without any ill effects," explains longtime woodpecker researcher Walter Koenig. "This is quite a feat given all the nasty defensive chemicals (tannins) that acorns contain."

Acorn Woodpecker families work together to store acorns and defend territories. Most surprising, females may mate with several other members of their group, and even lay their eggs in the same communal nest with other family females.

The system isn't problem-free. The first female to nest often has her egg broken open and devoured by other females. Not until each female has laid at least one egg do they all settle down for some serious chick-raising. When all the breeding males or females die within a group, there's also fierce competition to replace them from Acorn Woodpeckers outside of the family.

Woodpeckers rank right up there with nature's best parents. I watched these Three-toed Woodpecker parents for almost an hour and they never strayed far from their nest, which is partially hidden below that lichen-covered branch.

"The fights they have over reproductive vacancies within groups—we call them power struggles—can last for weeks," explains Walt Koenig. "They can involve nonstop fighting and vocalizations among dozens of birds, and are some of the most exciting things I've ever seen in nature."

But before you get the idea that Acorn Woodpeckers are the only woodpeckers that behave differently, let's take a quick look at some other woodpecker "bad birds" that like to break the rules…

Sapsuckers– Slurping Sap and Taking Names

I'll say it once more: all woodpeckers eat insects, but as you saw with Acorn Woodpeckers, some also have figured out tasty alternatives. If you've ever dripped maple syrup over a pancake, you can understand why sapsuckers prefer sap over all other foods. Tree sap is loaded with sugars that fuel a bird's energetic lifestyle.

"Sapsuckers have a paintbrush-like appearance on the end of their tongue," explains biologist Bret

◄ *The bird with perhaps the most fun name of any woodpecker, the Yellow-bellied Sapsucker.*

➤ Male Williamson's Sapsucker bringing ants to nest.

Tobalske. "This type of brushy structure helps them lap up sap." Each hole produces sap for three or four days, and the birds drill new holes in horizontal lines next to it.

Other species move in on the sap-slurping action. Downy, Red-headed, and Hairy Woodpeckers all slurp sap at sapsucker "wells"— along with Baltimore Orioles, nuthatches, and more warblers than you want to count. The sap wells may be especially important to hummingbirds. At least four kinds of hummingbirds have been seen feeding at sapsucker holes, and Ruby-throated Hummingbirds often build nests nearby.

One advantage to sap wells is that they also attract insects. In fact, Williamson's Sapsuckers depend on ants more than any other North American woodpecker. Often before devouring an ant or other insect, birds will dunk it in sap—an especially nice way to serve ants at your next sleepover!

Lewis's Woodpeckers– Eating on the Fly

Although few people have heard of a Lewis's Woodpecker, for scientists, the bird is royalty. Why? Because the first European Americans to see the bird were members of the Lewis and Clark Expedition and—as you've no doubt figured out—the woodpecker is named after the expedition's co-leader, Captain Meriwether Lewis. For biologists, however, the bird stands out for another reason.

"Lewis's Woodpeckers, unlike any of the other members of the Picidae family, are especially adapted for flycatching behavior," says scientist Megan Fylling. The birds sit on a promising perch and wait for a juicy insect to fly by. Then, they shoot after it like a tree-to-air missile. The Red-headed and several other woodpeckers attempt this "hawking" behavior but none master it like Lewis's. "They have very broad wings and are very maneuverable in the air, which allows them to catch their insect prey," Megan explains.

"Unfortunately, since they have evolved to be flycatching woodpeckers," Megan continues, "they have apparently lost sufficient cushioning in their heads to excavate their own nesting and roosting cavities unless it's in a tree that is already rotting." This means that the birds can live only where large, decaying trees are still standing.

➤ *Other woodpeckers occasionally "hawk" for insects in mid-air, but none has mastered it like Lewis's Woodpecker, as this incredible in-flight photo by Kate Davis shows! Lewis's beaks open wider than the beaks of other woodpeckers. This wider gape helps them snag insects in mid-air.*

Black-backed Woodpeckers–Burnin' Down the House

Within days of a forest fire, battalions of wood-boring beetles show up in the blackened forest. The beetles lay their eggs under the bark layers of the dead trees, and billions of beetle larvae hatch and begin munching their way into the dead wood. As the larvae begin to hatch, however, their worst nightmare swoops in to greet them—the Black-backed Woodpecker.

Black-backed Woodpeckers live almost entirely in burned forests with big dead trees still standing. "Wood-boring beetles are deeper than bark beetles," explains biologist Dick Hutto. "Most woodpeckers are getting bark beetles and stuff, but Black-backed woodpeckers are digging in deeper to get the bigger larvae. These are big juicy morsels. Greater reward. And the beetle populations go through

◄ *By nesting in woodpecker holes in burned forests, Mountain Bluebirds and many other bird species find both insect prey and safety from hungry squirrels, chipmunks, and other small mammals.*

the roof because the trees are defenseless once they're killed."

While they are drilling after beetles, of course, Black-backed Woodpeckers are also chiseling out nesting and roosting holes into the cement-hard wood. By doing so, they open up burned forests to other cavity-nesting species like Mountain Bluebirds, House Wrens, and Tree Swallows. With the help of the Black-backeds, these birds—and others—reach a higher abundance in severely burned forests than in any other kind of habitat. This makes Black-backeds one of America's most important forest birds—and, if you ask me, should replace Smokey Bear as the official mascot for the United States Forest Service!

Hot-Footed Fact

. . . .

Black-backed Woodpeckers are one of two kinds of three-toed woodpeckers in North America, the other being the American Three-toed Woodpecker. Both species have only three toes instead of the usual four toes found on other woodpeckers. Why? Your guess is as good as mine. Maybe they don't like "finger foods" as much as other woodpeckers!

Gila Woodpeckers– Showing Some Spine

If you're ever hiking through the Sonoran Desert, there's a good chance you'll spot a Gila Woodpecker. It won't be clinging to a tree like other woodpeckers. Instead, it'll be sitting on the most uncomfortable perch you can imagine—a large, spine-covered saguaro cactus.

Like most woodpeckers, Gila Woodpeckers feed on a variety of foods, but they have a special fondness for the pollen, fruit, and nectar of saguaros and other cactuses. You might guess that Gila Woodpeckers excavate nest holes in very large saguaros—and you'd be right! These holes are later used by Elf Owls and at least eight other native bird species. Relying on a single plant, though, can be risky. The spread of Phoenix, Tucson, and other desert cities has destroyed large expanses of saguaro "forests," reducing the habitat for this one-of-a-kind woodpecker.

And that prickly point brings me to a topic I'd rather not discuss at all…

◀ Gila Woodpecker feeding on fruits of a giant cactus in Saguaro National Park, Arizona.

Vanishing Woodpeckers

By now, I hope you're as blown away by woodpeckers as I am. No other birds that I know of do as much for the world or are as fun to study. Unfortunately, we humans haven't understood woodpeckers very well and have done some pretty stupid things that have harmed them. Two of the world's largest woodpeckers, the Ivory-billed Woodpecker and the Imperial Woodpecker, are both probably extinct. Both needed extensive old-growth forests full of large trees to live in, and logging, hunting, poisoning and other human activities spelled doom for these birds. Although hunting woodpeckers is no longer legal, many other woodpecker populations are declining—mostly because they are running out of places to live.

One problem is that humans don't like messy-looking landscapes. "If we had our way," explains Dick Hutto, "everything would be green trees, green lawns, and cement." But woodpeckers are telling us to appreciate the messy parts of nature.

"The Black-backed Woodpecker obviously is telling us something about how cool burned forests are," says Dick. "Same with the Lewis's Woodpecker. It's telling us how important big old dead rotten ugly cruddy

➤ *Like Acorn Woodpeckers, Red-cockaded Woodpeckers live in family groups that co-operate to raise their young.*

trees are on your land. And the same with all the other woodpeckers. Flickers bang on houses because they sound empty underneath, like rotten trees."

By looking through a woodpecker's eyes, we can understand nature better. We can also act to help protect these amazing birds—and the species that depend on them.

Red-cockaded Woodpeckers

Red-cockaded Woodpeckers are the only woodpeckers to nest in living pine trees. They once ranged through 90 million acres of longleaf pine forest in the eastern United States. During the nineteenth and twentieth centuries, however, 97% of this forest was logged or destroyed by human development. Not surprisingly, the woodpecker's population plunged from 1 to 1.6 million family groups to about 10,000 individual birds. In 1973, the bird was protected under the Endangered Species Act, but its recovery has been slow, and many groups of Red-cockaded Woodpeckers are still threatened or declining.

Lost Treasures?
Ivory-Billed and Imperial Woodpeckers

Up until the mid-twentieth century, North America's—and the world's—two largest woodpecker species were the Ivory-billed and the Imperial Woodpecker. The Ivory-billed lived in the southeastern United States and Cuba, while the Imperial Woodpecker lived in central Mexico. Both species thrived in very old forests full of giant trees, and they both fed on large beetle grubs. As loggers cleared the forests, the birds' numbers declined. Collectors shot large numbers of the birds while insecticides and other poisons may also have harmed them. The last reliable sightings of the Ivory-billed Woodpecker occurred in Cuba in the mid-1980s. The last solid report of the Imperial Woodpecker came from Mexico in the 1950s. Since then, scientists have searched extensively for survivors. Several people reported seeing Ivory-billed Woodpeckers in Arkansas in 2004, but most scientists believe these probably were Pileated Woodpeckers. The search continues, and many hold out hope that new populations of both species will be discovered.

➤ *Painting of Ivory-billed Woodpeckers by famous naturalist and artist John James Audubon.*

Speaking–and Acting– Up For Woodpeckers

Destruction of habitat is probably the Number One threat to woodpeckers. Woodpeckers need lots of dead, rotting trees because that's where they find insects to eat and make homes to live. If you live on a large piece of land, urge your parents to leave rotting logs and old dead standing trees—as long as they aren't about to fall down on your mom's new minivan or crush your kid brother!

If you live in an area with forest fires, write letters to your newspaper and your local representatives—including the Forest Service and private timber companies—urging them not to do salvage logging after a fire. Especially encourage them to leave the stands of larger dead trees that Black-backed and other woodpeckers depend on.

During the winter, if you'd like to help out your local Downy Woodpeck-

◄ Warning sign to hikers not to disturb nesting Red-cockaded Woodpeckers.

ers, Red-bellied Woodpeckers, or Northern Flickers, you can always put up a suet feeder in your yard. Just remember to take it down when temperatures start to warm up again. The grease from the suet can mess up a woodpecker's feathers—and cause other woodpeckers to laugh at it! While you're at it, keep your cats indoors to prevent them from killing woodpeckers and other birds around your house.

The most important thing you can do for woodpeckers is to educate your friends, family, and teachers about the importance of burned and "messy" forests. Teach them that there is beauty and value in all parts of nature—not just the neatly groomed and manicured parts. The woodpeckers will th-th-thank you for all your efforts.

And s-s-s-s-so do I.

▼ Suet may help Red-bellied and other woodpeckers make it through the winter in cold climates.

Now that you've, uh, penetrated the bark of the world of woodpeckers, I hope you'll want to chisel deeper. The best way, as always, is to observe these cool critters for yourself. Woodpeckers live in almost every part of North America. To help you locate local woodpeckers, look at the species maps on eBird (ebird.org/ebird/explore). You also can contact your local Audubon Society by visiting www.audubon.org and clicking on "Chapter Near You." Most local Audubon groups send out reports of bird sightings in their areas as well as offering bird-watching trips. If you go out, be sure to take along binoculars, a camera, and a bird guide such as my son's favorite, *The Sibley Guide to Birds*, or the one I usually carry, *Kaufman's Field Guide to Birds of North America*.

Another great resource is the Cornell Lab of Ornithology, which runs an excel-lent website called "All About Birds" that can help you learn more about woodpeckers and other bird species. You can find it at www.birds.cornell.edu. If you want to learn even more, you might subscribe to Birds of North America Online (bna.birds.cornell.edu/bna), where I gathered a lot of the information I included in this book. You can ask your local librarian if this service may be available for free through your library.

Unfortunately, there aren't many good children's books about woodpeckers, but if you want to learn more about the importance of burned forests to woodpeckers and other birds, I urge you to read my book *Fire Birds—Valuing Natural Wildfires and Burned Forests*. You can also probably find adult reference books about woodpeckers in your public and university libraries. Two fascinating adult books about the search for the Ivory-billed and Imperial Woodpeckers are *Imperial Dreams: Tracking the Imperial Woodpecker Through the Wild Sierra Madre* and *The Grail Bird: The Rediscovery of the Ivory-billed Woodpecker*, both by ornithologist Tim Gallagher. Check 'em out!

Once you start learning about woodpeckers, you won't want to stop. Woodpeckers are so fascinating that observing and learning about them is a journey that lasts a lifetime. The best advice I can give you is to get out there and enjoy the adventure!

◄ *Acorn Woodpecker feeding babies inside its telephone pole nest.*

Woodpecker Words

◀ *Pileated Woodpecker feeding chicks.*

long in woodpeckers and helps the birds extend their tongues great distances

ornithologist—a person who studies birds

retrices—stiff tail feathers that help support a bird clinging to the side of a vertical surface

roosting—resting or sleeping

sap well—several holes, drilled close to each other in a tree trunk, that are producing a flow of sap

snags—dead trees that are still standing

(bird) suet—a mixture of fat, nuts, fruit, and seeds intended for feeding birds

tannins—chemicals that often taste bitter and serve to defend plants against animals that eat them

cavity nester—an animal that nests in a hole, usually in a tree trunk

communal nest—a nest shared by more than one female

conifer forests—forests composed of pine, fir, spruce and other cone-bearing trees

deciduous forests—forests full of trees that lose their leaves every fall

flycatch—the ability to snatch insects out of the air

gape—the distance an animal's mouth or beak can open wide

granaries—food storage locations for woodpeckers

hawking—hunting by sitting on a perch, then darting out to catch insects and other prey in mid-air (see "flycatch")

hyoid bone—a bone that aids in the movement of the tongue; it is especially

▲ *Fledgling Hairy Woodpecker about to head off to college.*

43

◄ One of our most seldom-seen woodpeckers, White-headed Woodpeckers live only at high altitudes in far-west mountain ranges of the United States and Canada.

Th-th-th-thanks!

Excavating this book took several years, and I wouldn't have been able to tackle it without a flock of great helpers. I'd like to thank Dick Hutto for first teaching me about woodpeckers and showing me what incredible creatures they are, and also for offering excellent suggestions and corrections on the manuscript before publication. Loud drum rolls, too, for the significant contributions of other woodpecker experts including Megan Fylling, Walter Koenig, Vicki Saab, and Bret Tobalske. I especially thank my son, Braden Collard, for helping me find wild woodpeckers and tolerating my endless obsession with them, as well as taking excellent woodpecker photos featured in this book. As always, my daughter, Tessa, and wife, Amy, bolstered me with their unflagging support and confidence while I continued to peck away at this project. Another special thank you to Larry Pringle for helping me ambush Red-bellied Woodpeckers and Yellow-bellied Sapsuckers in his backyard, and last, I thank my terrific designer, Kathy Paoli, for melding words and art into a book that I hope will, like woodpeckers, stand the test of time.

About the Author

Sneed B. Collard III graduated with Honors in biology from the University of California at Berkeley, and has written more than eighty books for young people and adults. His recent award-winning titles include *Fire Birds—Valuing Natural Wildfires and Burned Forests; Catching Air—Taking the Leap with Gliding Animals;* and *Hopping Ahead of Climate Change—Snowshoe Hares, Science, and Survival,* which was a finalist for the Green Earth Book Award and the AAAS/Subaru/Science Books & Films Prize for Excellence in Science Books. To write *Woodpeckers,* Sneed and his son Braden spent four years observing and photographing woodpeckers in North and South America. To learn more about Sneed, his books, and author visits, explore his website at www.sneedbcollardiii.com and follow Sneed and Bucking Horse Books on Facebook.

➤ *The author and his son, Braden, scouting for woodpeckers in the Sonoran Desert.*

Woodpecker Photo Bloopers

Hopefully, you've enjoyed the clear, sharp photographs of woodpeckers featured in this book, but wanna know a secret? For every great photo I or another photographer takes, we take about a hundred horrible ones—images that just don't quite make the grade for a book like this. My son, Braden, and I thought it would be fun to share a few of these bloopers—especially of woodpeckers we didn't feature elsewhere in the book. Enjoy!

⋏ NUTTALL'S WOODPECKER

One of our least-known woodpeckers, Nuttall's lives only in California and northern Baja California—but just try getting one to pose in full sunlight!

⋏ ➤ ARIZONA WOODPECKERS

With their chocolate brown feathers, Arizona Woodpeckers are some of the prettiest North American woodpeckers, but boy did we have a hard time photographing them! Here are the best photos we could manage—curse all sticks and bushes!

➤ SCARLET-BACKED WOODPECKER

Only a few feet from where we saw the Black-cheeked Woodpecker in Ecuador (see page 18), this spectacular guy landed in a neighboring tree. Again, curse all sticks and shadows!

⌄ CRIMSON-CRESTED WOODPECKER

Have you ever heard Carol King's song "So Far Away"? Probably not, huh? Anyway, this Crimson-crested Woodpecker is a case in point. But at least there's a Many-banded Aracari in the picture, too!

Index

◀ *Andean Flicker*